RAMBO/RIMBAUD

Catherine Bull

"Poetry will no longer
accompany action, but will lead it."

— Arthur Rimbaud

Table of Contents

Filling Station (Rambo & Rimbaud, Proprietors)

A thoroughly dirty
little gas station
on a high desert road,
oil-soaked, oil-permeated
to an overall
mirage translucency
under the bored stare
of an afternoon which asks, if,
since things are so slow,
could it go early?

Rimbaud sits in the shade
of the cement porch
behind the pumps
on a crushed and grease-
impregnated wickerwork taboret,
part of a set,
beside a big hirsute begonia.
He wears a bowler hat
and a dirty, oil-soaked monkey suit, too large,
and rolled at the legs
and the arms into fat cuffs.
He is struggling
to remove his boots.
The taboret creaks

1

underneath him
as if it needs *more* oil.

Rambo sits on the dirty
wicker sofa, sharpening
a large black knife.
It slides along the whetstone,
back along the whetstone,
along the whetstone,
back along the whetstone.
A comfy shushing.
His oil-soaked monkey suit
strains across his pectorals
and cuts into his jugular,
an indentation in danger
of becoming permanent.

He also wears a bowler hat.
His has a red band,
the only note
of certain color
in the station.
Even the daisy stitch
and marguerites on the big
dim doily draping the low back
of the wicker sofa
are heavy with oil.
Or were perhaps

crocheted out of it.
Rambo stands, unzips his monkey suit
halfway and ties the arms
together at the waist.
His scarred chest gleams
like it's been oiled.
He does push-ups.

Rimbaud writes lists
on sheets of Your Co. Name
notepad paper,
the ballpoint slipping
across little rosettes of grease.

A hundred says Rambo.
A hundred and one.

The old neon sign spits
ESSO—SO—SO—SO
at its proprietors.

———————

The sun dawns like a tossed coin
landing heads after coming up every time tails.

Rambo slowly settles
his bowler hat

firmly, with both hands,
onto his head. The muscles
in his back and biceps quilt.

Rimbaud clumps, his boots
sticking out their tongues,
around back of the station.
There's a pale and shredded
tarpaulin lean-to
strung with spent light sticks
tied up with bits of shoelace.
Inside the lean-to everything
is mildew, mildew, mildew.
And parked catacorner
an ancient mini pickup truck,
its original color dubious.

———————————————————

Rambo and Rimbaud
push the mini pickup
up to the top of a nearby rise.

With Rambo in the driver's seat
the little truck rolls backward
towards the station.
Rambo steers it
right at the pump island,
diving out of the cab

at the dire moment.
He hustles up the hill,
losing and retrieving
his bowler hat in the process.

Rimbaud upends a duffel
with three good shakes.
A bow drops. An arrow.
The greasy doily and a Zippo.
He flicks open the Zippo
and flips it shut,
flicks it open and flicks it shut.

Rambo wraps the tip of the arrow
in the doily and Rimbaud,
with ceremony, lights it.

Rambo notches the arrow
and aims, the gasoline
from the knocked-over pumps
misting upright
and wisping sideways.
He lets the arrow
with a snapping twang,
quite musical, fly.

Across the ground
a pulled thread, electric blue,

molts into flames,
low and peach-colored.
The sprays of gasoline
catch and thicken, rising twinned, orange and
blood orange,spiraling askew
with infinite spongey flame.
And then at last—oh
but it is loud!
a rampant overlap of kablooeys.

Toasty heat
embraces the hill,
though the smell is acrid
and makes their nostrils sting
and their eyes water.
The roiling plumage
of the filling station,
moil bearable to no one
but from afar, blown up,
and blowing up.

Will they open a new station?
They might stick out their thumbs
at the nearest crossroads.
Where could they go?
Somewhere there is
a place for them.
For somewhere there is a place for us all.

Rambo
& The Lice Women

Under the slow surging
and retreating
of my desire to go back
an old harmonica pushes
its sigh somewhere.
The liquor of hope wells up
but drowns in my eyes.

Under the seasoned, indifferent fingers
of the charming, indistinct sisters, the crackle
and pop of the little lice dying
resounds as one pulsing
electric finger then another
move to crush.

Blue air spits flowers
through the window they have jimmied
open with their long, knife fingers.

I hear mascara beating.
I hear lips sucking saliva
through fissures I paid to kiss.
I try to breathe
to the sing-song,

their delicate, wicked fingers
advancing through my heavy curls
and combing away the dead.

Dreams swarm, beg.
They smell of old roses.
They call me honey.
They take me to the bed.

I shrug them off.
Frowning, I tear a headband
from the red bedclothes
and secure my torments.

Rambo's Bohemia

And so I left, my fists tearing new pockets
in a coat made of bullet holes.
The sweaty blue sky ordered me to dream
and I asked how high!

Appleseed, John J. In ripped fatigues
I scattered handfuls of blood
no matter where I tried to go.
Homeless most nights, I watched my stars
slide across the whetstone sky.

On heavy evenings the rain fell, ringing
like spent machine gun shells in the heat, a
lullaby I swallowed.

And there, in the midst of expendable shadows,
as if they were bow strings I'd pluck the laces
of my scarred boots, my foot pointed at my
                                                    heart.

Rambo On Rimbaud

What he's trying to do is change what is.
Spilled his guts and gave everything he had,
the whole picture –
look how big he wrote.
He wrote to win, to survive.

Oh yeah, I'm serious.
I've always believed
the mind is the best weapon
and you just don't turn it off—I'm no tourist.
What he calls hell I call home,
alone through the minefield.

Got a compass? 'Cause nothing does change and
there isn't one of us that doesn't want to be
someplace else.

It's a long story, it's a knife, it's a blue light,
it's all this junk in the pocket, it's Lone Wolf
calling Wolf Den,
kind of like a quiet war,
the kind of war you don't die for,
and what are you going to do about it?
"Get a couple beers
and look at the road," he wrote,
"Look at the boat."

I can't put it out of my mind,
he said, "Us as much as we."
Pieces of him all over me.
Father, maybe. I don't know.
Maybe just a little.
"Fuck the world. Go home.
Fuck you. Come back."
He said, "Live for nothing."
Or he said "life is nothing."

The boat will be waiting.
And if it's not there
you can follow the shoreline.
So man the gun and keep moving.
Fire off a shot. Get 'em.
And go, go go go.

Rimbaud: First Blood

*A re-telling of the first Rambo film using lines
and phrases from Rimbaud's poems and letters*

I. Vagabond
*Rimbaud, a decorated veteran travels a forested
highway on foot*

I am the wanderer
along the main road, pale
from the hard kiss of freedom,
recovering from the old
fanfares of heroism which still
attack my heart and my head.
My fatal awkwardness. For weeks
my boots have been torn
by the pebbles on the road,
by my nameless ills.

With no disgust for the coffin,
my hungers are bits of black air.
The air and world
not sought after. Life. My life
does not weigh enough.
A smoking heap, the dead
in my belly drum, dance,
dance, dance, stamping
and stamping their twisted feet.

A pillow is over my mouth.
They cannot hear me.

In sunlight without deception
what must a man do? I have no position except
continuous trouble.

I remember silvery hours and sun near rivers,
the hand of the country on my shoulder,
the fiery fields, the friend
who was neither strong nor weak,
the friend to divert the enchantments and bawling
unspeakable songs and our nostrils full
of air and if you laughed in my face
I would have killed you.
Far from the former assassins
it is quite desolate. My eye is darkened.
It will not give the impression of a legend.

There are only fir-trees and ferns
on the mountain, stones looking up.
Impossible to express that flat daylight
produced by this unchanging sky.
The town isn't far.

I have no idea where I will be
in a month. That is fine.
I don't intend to stay here very long.
I did not find what I thought I would find.

II. Hope
Rimbaud encounters the Sheriff, and the Sheriff's
familiar opinions

The supremely stupid provincial town.
A stain of populace where the bellies
of basset dogs navigate peacefully in the twilight.
Sweet perennial vignettes, sweet
as sugar on bad teeth.
What monsters of innocence
these peasants are.

And then there's the someone
who chases you off
when you're hungry and thirsty,
the Sentinel saying "Idle youth
are loathsome to us.
Your life here would be a real torture.
The most boring place in the world."

This hardly makes me miss the world,
these shapes repeating themselves.

He says "Also? Your breath
warms stinkingly.

Let nothing put you off
sublime retreat."

The malice in attentiveness
deporting tyrannical codes of honesty.
I stick out my tongue,
my two fists. Let me go
where I wanted! These hands
have not sold oranges.
These hands have not washed the diapers
of heavy babies, they are not hands
of a cousin. They are benders of backbones.

I spring back into the dance
to the singing of bones.
Mad anger drives me toward battle.
A crime, quick! so I can be dropped
into the void, turned over to justice
in accordance with the law of man.

He says "Put down the bundles."

III. Jail
Shabby treatment, flashbacks, escape

Punishment! Naked from top to bottom.
Hell for the offenders his palm

has frisked and while waiting for the few small
acts of cowardice still to come – never delirium
and torture like this. How idiotic.
Sweated obedience to bitter hypocrisy –
is the voice of thought more than a dream?

A vaudeville conjures up horrors before me.
My hates, my fixed torpors,
my failings and my brutalities suffered
long ago – you give all back to me.
Red torments in a bamboo hut,
shutters closed, moldy hangings,
warm excrement, quivers of shutters, the buzzing,
the flag of red meat, mucus of azure, feet
on the rickety rail I saw myself
overcome with dizziness and hurled
down into the most horrible darkness.

The terrifying swiftness
of form and action when they are perfect!
The collapse of grace joined
with new violence! My great mad skeleton
carried off by my impetus
like a horse rearing!

You could say, as they turn about
in dark skirmishes, the minions are stiff knights
clashing cardboard armor,
apiece of flesh loose on their chins.

Slapping their heads with a backhand blow
makes it dance, dance! And the jostled puppets
entwine their thin arms.

I speak as comprehensibly as any wretch!
I took arms against justice.
I ran away.

IV. Chase

The Sheriff and his posse attempt recapture

I free myself
and fly off, covered up with the cold sweat
of the moon and verdure.
Heavy ocherous skies
and soaked forests.

Blood-spotted, whirling,
boughs breaking among red rustlings.
I am weak! Others
are advancing.

"You will remain a hyena...etc!"
yells the demon who crowned me,
"Come down here, that I can whip you!"

Tools, weapons...time!

Men from huge desks, bloated,
their skulls caked with vague roughness,
their fists sunken in soiled cuffs,
think about those who made them get up
from under the warm blanket and argue
over what they are totally ignorant of.
Out of shape, bunches of tonsils
under their meager chins tremble
and almost burst. When darkness
drools in the woods like a cow's muzzle
they go off, taking their dogs on the leash.
Shit to those dogs!

I shudder at the passing
of hunts and hordes, the firing squad,
the terrible irony.

V. Fall

A deputy corners Rimbaud and attempts murder,
with deadly results

An amphitheater crowned with foliage, a frightful
                                        rock
where a river falls everywhere,
avalanches of water like champagne bubbles
whose angle is struck by whirls of light.

Tremblings rise and threaten.

Distances cataract toward the abyss.

An underling, swarthy,
stupid brain teeming with nits
– in short, morals and speech
reduced to their simplest expression –
in his half-drunked indolence
the asshole with the whip makes me leap,
his lips bursting with laughter.

Under a flood of daylight falling
I sink, eating air, I can't cry out
and everything grows
and everything rises
a minute or months on end
the hour of my death holding wide open
its splendors.

A clock which doesn't strike!
Alive and breaking
through the exquisite tapestry of the great trees
with a heavy thud, gashes
on my entire body, it is over.
It is a good joke. And the world jeers.

And I am not lucky. A gust of wind
makes operatic cracks,
confuses the pivoting and throws down
through the fiendish and billowy silence

the low idiot.
The birds cry at once.
The ferns bend their heads.

He is deader than a fossil.

All the infinitely pale reflections
stir. His back is broken,
purple gums, the dark moss, organs
spread everywhere in the silk water.
Detestable to the highest degree,
the visitation of memories.

I beg you, Sentinel! Show a less glaring eye.
I have not committed evil. He fell
from the blue heights in criminal air.
Without being dazed let us
evaluate the extent of my innocence.
But a ray of light gilds his shoulder,
the errant knight.

VI. Hunt

*The Sheriff and posse fail to match wits with
Rimbaud*

"A serious danger for society,"
says the Sentinel.

So ardent Justice comes
in the burping nights.

The panting idiots, the old men, the puppets,
the lackeys leaping about.
Stay-at-homes, suckers of short pipes,
eaters of soup hurl themselves about
and in low voices (they are cunning!)
say to one another, "What does it matter for us?"

I hear your black eyelashes beating.
Silence between my teeth,
a blade in my hands, I am hidden
and I am not hidden.
There is no one here and
there is someone.

I possess every talent.
Up now! be ballerinas for me
for one moment.
I would like to break your hips.

And when you are down, moaning
on your guts, when all the trembling wood
bleeds, one smells
how the earth is nubile
and rich in blood.

Head in arms, knees to teeth

in the heart of black fissures
bled black, faces deformed, ashen.
Pale with black scent,
scarlet and black wounds break out
on the proud flesh.
Whistles and rings
of muffled music: moans,
sniffles and whispers.

I pounce stealthily.
It has been found again.
What has? – Eternity.
This expense
and this futile disorder.

Pock-marked, his eyes
circled with green rings, his swollen
fingers clenched on his thighbones
and eyes protruding – his curses rain down
stronger than alcohol. At times a hiss
interrupts, saliva caught on the lip
lain with his inviolate hate.

On the nape, placing my crossed hands...
and the poor troublemaker
in very seriously clownish hiccoughs
all scared to death
writes an epitaph for himself.

Ah, let him go off! with his throat
wearing a necktie of shame.
I have said what I intended to.

Let me follow the roads
here again, hat, coat, my two fists
in my pocket, answering questions
and coarse evil apostrophies by silence.
Let me keep away from justice.

VII. Commander

Rimbaud's old commanding officer, the Colonel,
explains to the posse who they're dealing with, and
addresses Rimbaud across the forest night

"And he especially savored dark things,
strange, unfathomable,
repulsive, delicious things. Odors
do not make his nostrils quiver.
He exhausts all poisons
in himself and keeps only their quintessences.
No other soul would have enough strength –

strength of despair – to endure it.
You are making a mistake."

From the same wilderness
in the same night, my tired eyes,

my closed eyes see spots.

"He will not go away, he will not
come down again, he will not
redeem the anger. He will
attach a new garland of hanged men
to the arms of the forest.
'Alive or dead?' Count on this:
it will cost you plenty."

A black powder gently rains
on my night, fine powder.

———

"Is it in these bottomless nights
that you sleep and exile yourself?"

Minor chords cross
one another and diminish.

"You would be loathsome
not to answer. Quickly.
Come back, everything will be forgotten.
What are you going to do?
All the capital sins?"

If brass wakes up a trumpet
it is not its fault.

"A town you can't find,
because it sees wandering about in its streets
two or three hundred soldiers.
Retired grocers clothed in their uniforms
are a terrible spectacle!
Come, we will put off
the return of fire. If you heed this,
you will show courage
and sincerity."

I understand, thought
holding onto thought and pulling,
and not knowing how
to explain this – I prefer to be silent.

VIII. Mine

Weekend warriors trap Rimbaud in an abandoned
mine and blow up the entrance

As I faced the gracious twisting
of the two pronounced arches
a shudder shook, the clock of life
stopped just now. The floors
and the enormous ceiling beams jut out
crazily as if to kiss each other.
I am no longer in the world.

I am absolutely thwarted, lost
in the foliage of caves
far underground, far from birds,
herds and village girls, at my side nothing
but the thickness of the globe,
the plaque of the black earth
full of strange stridor, the limpid song of new woe
caught in a horrible funnel.

Here forms, sweating, hair and eyes,
floating corridors of black gauze.
Inspecting the invisible
and hearing the unheard,
I will have to face the sly rat
and plaster with painful blisters
the blue feelings of disgust.

At a tremendous distance
above my subterranean room
those wretches go off, the good soldiers
get up politely in confusion
with the sheets of fog
spaced in horrible bands in the sky
which bends back. How lively they are,
notaries, glaziers, tax-collectors,
carpenters and all the fat-bellied dignitaries
with rifles over their hearts, drunk
on great names. Syphilitics, fools,
idlers, monkey-hawkers, red-headed

troop of hip wrigglers
not worthy to untie my laces.
Dragging my wings after me
in the shadows, enormity
becoming normal – my last regrets
scamper off.

The wind laden with sounds, there!
a very small patch,
the still delicate hour
pinned up by a naughty star, small
and very white in a constantly swelling
crowd of dark ghosts rising up in my veins,
the flood of living worms.

My two cents worth of reason is over.
What is my void,
compared with the stupefaction
awaiting you?

IX. Drinks

*The Sheriff and the Colonel, believing Rimbaud to
be dead in the mine, have a drink*

The Sentinel: "Some golden liquor
                     that brings on sweat?
                     My day is done."

The Officer: "Untaxed liquor?
                  In the hope of better weather."

The Sentinel: "May it come may it come.
                  Worth the excrement of a
                  sea bird, you know."

The Officer: "Alcohol as strong
                  as boiling metal?"

The Sentinel: "No, the obdurate convict!
                  Whom Death, lofty mistress,
                  has sown."

The Officer: "Your serene tenderness
                  blows in the night like a
                  whale. What an old maid I
                  am becoming, in lacking the
                  courage to love death."

The Sentinel: "I have my duty and I am
                  unable to understand revolt.
                  I know what happens
                  happens and that is all."

The Officer: "You reserve your place
                  at the top of the ladder
                  of angelic common sense."

The Sentinel: "We go where we don't want
                   to go and do what we don't
                   want to do, and live and die
                   differently than we would l
                   like, without hope for any
                   kind of compensation—
                   the farce we all play.
                   These ferocious invalids,
                   asking for the mercy
                   of daylight..."

The Officer: "He was the first who went in.
                   Lively, hot-headed, often

                                            angry
                   and having no patience for
                   things he didn't like.
                   He was almost a child."

The Sentinel: "A delightful youth, heroic
                   and fabulous. The Great
                   What's-His-Name!
                   And the mother, closing the
                   exercise book, goes off
                   satisfied and very proud."

The Officer: "They have no mothers."

The Sentinel: "Their souls begin

accidentally?"

The Officer: "More of these pure drinks."

The Sentinel: "In a terrible way I insist
                      on worshipping free freedom,
                      neither joke nor paradox."

The Officer: "Freed, they are like dogs:
                      people insult them.
                      Enslaved by a defeat with
                      no future. And only cold
                      scorn is left. He did not
                      return, and will never return.
                      He will never tell us what he
                      knows and what we will
                      never know. This does not
                      mean nothing."

The Sentinel: "Listen to you,
                      making infamy into glory,
                      cruelty into charm. The
                      world marches on! No more
                      thens. *Your* heart
                      beats in that abdomen."

The Officer: "We got on together."

The Sentinel: "But that is no concern of

                                    mine..
                    He attacks me, and makes me
                    spend hours
                    humiliated like a whipped dog.
                    What was I saying to you?"

The Officer: "Dung on the daisy.
                    The first dog in the street
                    will tell you so."

The Sentinel: "I miss the days of ancient
                                                youth.
                    Let's move on.
                    No more vagabonds."

The Officer: "No more vague wars."

X. Destruction
Violent revenge is served

Can man reach ecstasy in destruction
and be rejuvenated by cruelty?

Hard night. The field
given over to oblivion.
The dried blood smokes,
slowly spreading my shoulder blades,

o rage! Spotted with dark streaks,
my cheeks look hollow.
Without noise the pale night
coagulates, evening grows
dark like a burning aquarium.
An unhealthy thirst
darkens in my veins.

No more of these landscapes.
Showers of gasoline, dizziness,
crumblings, routs and pity – the world's heart
endlessly burned. It is so beautiful!
The redness of bombs
in frenzy on the reddened walls
raise up the black specters of the roofs, ardent
and full of dark misfortune.
It is too beautiful!

Trumpeting and brandishing my grievance
the blazing fires stream
in the frosty gusts, running
like a thief from window to window.

A large scythe of light
on frightful smashed door-locks. The moon
burns and shouts.

The air swollen with impalpable veils of smoke
illuminated endlessly. Fears and suffering

have not undergone a more triumphant hubbub!
Victory is mine.

I don't remember farther back
than the wound that never heals.
What was the language I spoke?
At what latitude?
Like the fire-flowers, red pigeons
thunder around my thought
snarling monstrosities, yelling threnodies.

To relieve the bitter need I call
to my executioners to let me
bite the ends of their guns.

XI. Over
Despair, guidance from the Colonel,
and partial understanding

I am certain that I smell scorched.
Neither country nor friends,
not a friendly hand!
I don't know what to do.

"Although it is frightful
to see you again covered thus;
although one has never
made of a city an ulcer

more foul-smelling on green nature,
come...the sufferings are enormous
but one has to be strong.
Far from the old places
and the old fire we hear
and smell all the possibilities
of harmony and architecture.
It's as simple as a musical phrase.
Invent new flames, new stars,
new flesh, new tongues."

Heaven! Love! Freedom! What a dream,
sweeter than the flesh
of hard apples is to children,
to work proudly all day
listening to duty like the sound of a trumpet.
The blasts of the heavy trumpet burn
inside me, and my sad heart,
frightened by a bullfinch!
is always fitting to lock the door.
And the numberless terrors
which sing, na-na, always burying
my joy like black gravel –
I am cursed, you know!
The evenings, mornings,
nights, days. How tired I am!
Cool my brow, if you will,
if only you will.

Worms in my hair and armpits
and still bigger worms in my heart,
the persistent taste
sadder than mourning.
The thousand bereavements,
those thousand questions, a million souls
and dead bodies which will be judged.
We aren't serious when we're seventeen!
Through what crime, through what error
did I deserve my present weakness?
Here there is no hope, dead
to good and this is still life!
And damnation is eternal.
Surging in me and dying
continuously a desire to cry.

Let me lift up with a withered fist
the coffin's lid, and sit down.

"Are you going to be carried off
like a child to play in Paradise
and forget all misfortune?
A spiritual battle is as brutal
as a battle of men, the yoke
which weighs on the soul and the brow
of all humanity. What will happen
to the world when you leave it?

Nothing, in any case. What is rotten
must be thrown aside."

Rotting things germinate.

"Your worms, your pale worms
will no more impede your breath
of progress than the white swarm
of indistinct dreams – what soul
is without flaws?"

Tremblings rise and threaten
and the persistent taste of these effects
combines with the whistle of men
and the discordant music
coming from castles of bones.
The dark past crumbling,
giving its death-rattle,
not fixed and not forced –
in my mind I have roads –
my boots torn
by the pebbles on the roads.

"There are no roads or even paths there,
where sleep the dead of yesterday.
Yes! Our life is a misery,
an endless misery!
Why do we exist?
To sweep away those

millions of skeletons?
All our embracing is but a question.
Amass in your heart
sugary spit and white tears, boiling.
Eat the rocks that are broken.
Dance, dance, dance, dance
all the tarantellas! No violent decisions
about salvation. The world
is ageless. Humanity simply moves about."

This poison will still
be in my veins, the sighs
of the nights when the heart bleeding
lets flow without witness its cryless revolt.

"Finish the story of your hell, it was
really hell, the old hell.
There is not real torture
in the fact that the suffering is sure."

I will get used to it?

"The blueness of dawn buzzes,
and that is heartening, is it not?
There is not real torture in the fact
that the suffering is sure."

The circulation of unknown saps,
old wives' remedies and rearranged popular songs

suddenly dyeing the blueness, weakness
or strength. Let us go now.

"Let us go now."

The Drunken Helicopter

I know the exquisite and terrible planets bulging
in the blackness, not just the orchid spots of
Mars, but I will never again try to feint, to open
fire, or even dream of rousing up devils of dust,
rising, magnificently backlit, over the horizon.

The enemy had jerked my Rambos out high over
broken fields, and when all their open mouths
had thudded shut in poofs of dust my dials
dizzied and I drifted like a child's tragic balloon
through fields of cauliflower clouds. I strafed
them in a fit of lightheading pique. Pistoned into
a thunderstorm's burgeoning hullabaloo, ten
times Hiroshima held in by tufts, clapped deafer
than mortal fear, for days the trampolining
hailstones scoured me clean of blood and
insignia. Up through the veils, and gravity's
fingers slipped from my runners.

Then the Poem of the Universe uncorked with a
wet squeak.

I took a swig and forgot all about tarmac and
loam. I drank more verses and my dull metal
sang auroras. Freed and on fire I could count a
million million fast as twenty—a million million

balls of dirty ice, a million million years.

As if I were an island, messages rippled my way,
the fears and fetishes of billions of gossipers, but
I outran that tsunami and sailed on, drowned
galaxies sinking in my wake. The cosmos
brought me carcasses of earlier voyagers but I
traveled on, mourning like a brass band second
line.

I swam behind moons bobbing like lost glass
fishing floats in a curve around a breaching
whale's horizon. I saw orbiting planets tilling
fields of stars, saw stars through other fields
stampede like hysterical cows. I safaried the
savannah where ancient and implausible animals
jiggling with fleas cross paths in rutting moods
and flash their teeth, and the archer hangs
grenades from his belt. I met stunted stars, unlit
fuses hanging in pinned sleeves. I saw
constipations of ice, tides of rock spasmed
through fissures, comets darting through the tips
throat-flaying seas.

Sometimes I wearied of the endless unfamiliar
beauty. And I'd have liked to show my Rambos
the suns gnawing paisleys in the black, the
insomniac suns. A deserter Crusoed, I fell as

hammering blackness beat them to tiny points.

Now lost, pulled into unknown depths and
captured in orbit, my rotors aimlessly
honeycombing a burled moon's airless sky—my
presence will never be predicted by astronmers'
math, my pockmarks will remain unnamed. I, I
who touched my skids to Saturn's rings and
played Immovable Blues without skipping, I
quiver for the guidance of human hands!
Vigorous future, where are you hiding? Olly-
olly-in-come-free, over…

It is over. This moon is too bright, this day rises
like bile. I still long for the company of a
soldier, but only for the child with a red necktie
around his head, alone under a maple, machine-
gunning seedpods with a stick as they helicopter
down.

Rimbaud On Rambo III

All the red stained mouths of machine guns ring
across the endless sky he paints with gasoline.
(I suspect this will lead to an abridgement
of my existence.) He flees like a squirrel
and blood laughs in our veins.
Morals and language, in short, reduced
to their simplest terms at last.
Master of silence, who sparks a blue blaze in a
                                        cave,
Rambo will never tell us what he knows.
His heart, his soul, all his strength
stupidly marches toward death
as if it were a terrible and fatal grace.

Clear sky! love! liberty! What dreams.
He is a banner of meat
that bleeds mere bouquets of flesh
scattered one petal at a time.
Belching bullets tear through flesh.
The eyes ignite, the blood sings,
the bones broaden, networks of scarlet –
the cadavers of the wicked
and slothful enemy fall
upon the hearts of no one.

Can man be in ecstasies over destruction

and through cruelty grow younger?
Two red holes in his right side.
He is no more likely
to be killed, of course, than a corpse.

But this strange suffering
holds an uncomfortable authority.
One can't help but sincerely desire that this soul,
which has strayed into our midst,
and wishes, apparently, death
(is it a battle or is it a dance
where a bad dream rattles?)
may in the end find comfort and consolations
and be worthy of them.

The Vagabonds (Now Mortgage-Bound)

Rambo and Rimbaud are living out their golden
                                        years
together in a house on the coast
with ropes and buoys decorating the deck.
It is situated along the beachy edge of things
among the tri-colored corrugated shacks
and the Airstreams parked in deer clearings
and the sleeps-15 vacation rental homes
with private ocean access and the single-wides
with four plastic pickets keeping back some
                                        geraniums
and one tall hotel, as if someone
had upended a Monopoly board,
taken all the paper money and left.
The ocean's pound and roar sounds to Rambo
like a warehouse full of men
shouting bets at stick fighters,
a bout no one will ever be able to end.
Rimbaud feels a dark affinity with the waves'
regularly thwarted decision to leave for good.
They are known as the Rimbaud, short-i hard-d
Rimbaud brothers, old Johnny and old Art.

When tavern talk in the Sea Hags Three or

                                        Andy's
turns as it will to regional legends
Rambo's law enforcement imbroglio
up in Hope, Washington comes up
along with D.B. Cooper and the time Jane Fonda
painted a peace sign naked in a traffic circle
near Fort Lewis. But he hardly resembles
                                    himself now.
He wears his gray hair short
atop the slow landslide of his face,
and he's recently had a penchant
for fine-knit sweaters, slacks and penny loafers.

And the schools are small
and not very good so no one is reading
nineteenth century hallucinatory French verse.
Art's pretty sure some kids
have stumbled on Patti Smith
and gotten suspicious but they are the ones
who leave behind the honeybee-keeping
jazz-flautist fathers and the entrepreneurial
waitress mothers and the goddamn-it-
I-got-it grandparents and the eager artist
                                    transplants
making a go of it at the farmer's market
to read alone, standing over dinner at the kitchen
                                        counter,
the letters Art writes religiously

to the county gazette's opinion page.
Dear Idiots, they begin, Dear Morons.

Since he funds and arranges the fireworks
every Fourth, all his letters are published.
He lets Johnny handle by himself
the pyrotechnics on the barge
anchored off the promontory,
ascetic Johnny who only gets drunk
on his own sweat. He is meditatively indifferent
to his old work the rest of the year,
except for the Fourth, when the 364 days
tick down to 00:00:00
and he can run amongst explosions again
and exhaust his body and his desire
without the burden of real carnage.

————————

Every few months they drive half a day to the
                                nearest city
big enough to really be called one
and go dancing at the Zanzibar.
Johnny wears a navy-blue cashmere turtleneck
tight over riptides of muscle
his face swims parallel to.
Art wears a thin old t-shirt

that matches his pale blue eyes
which sweep the dance floor
with lighthouse purpose.

The dancers swim through bullets of light
streaking from turning globes.
The jettisoned and the shy
sway around the edges like kelp.

Old Johnny dances taut as a bow string,
                                    crouching
and disappearing, rising in a burst.
Old Art's arms flick his fingers away
as if they were lice
and he moves this thigh
then this other thigh and this left leg.

Johnny always tries to resist, then rescue
someone else's Colonel.
Art always tries to insult and intoxicate
someone else's Verlaine.
But it is not the same. It's true
the tide brings back everything it takes.
But not back to you.

So they drive back home alone
together and sit on the dark beach
stiffening up

until like plastic toy figures
only one joint in each limb will bend.

ACKNOWLEDGEMENTS

Thank you to the editors of the journals in which these poems first appeared (sometimes in a different version):

Beatdom:
"Rambo's Bohemia"
"The Drunken Helicopter"

Bellingham Review:
"The Vagabonds,
Now Mortgage-Bound"

The Operating System:
"Filling Station
(Rambo & Rimbaud, Proprietors)"

The character of John Rambo was created by David Morrell in his 1972 novel *First Blood,* and continued in *First Blood* (screenplay) by Sylvester Stallone and David Giler; *First Blood II: The Mission* (draft screenplay) by James Cameron; *Rambo: First Blood Part II* (screenplay) by Sylvester Stallone and James Cameron; *First Blood Part II* (film novelization) by David Morrell; *Rambo III* (screenplay) by Sylvester Stallone and Sheldon Lettich; *Rambo III* (novelization) by David Morrell; and *Rambo* (screenplay) by Sylvester

Stallone and Art Monterastelli.

I am indebted to the following translators of Rimbaud's poems and letters: Daisy Aldan, Stanley Applebaum, John Ashbery, J. Norman Cameron, William M. Davis, Angel Flores, Kate Flores, Wallace Fowlie, Francis Golffing, Kenneth Koch and Georges Guy, Bert M-P Leefmans, Wyatt Mason, Claire Mcallister, Frederick Morgan, Enid Peschel, Paul Schmidt, Martin Sorrell, Stephen Stepanchev, Louise Varese, Vernon Watkins.

Epigraph: Arthur Rimbaud in a letter to Paul Demeny dated May 15th, 1871 (translation: Louise Varese).

"Filling Station (Rambo & Rimbaud, Proprietors)" is of course making liberal reference to "Filling Station" by Elizabeth Bishop.

"Rambo on Rimbaud" is a collage of phrases from Rambo dialogue in the above-listed books and screenplays.

"Rimbaud: First Blood" is a collage of lines and phrases from Arthur Rimbaud's letters and poems, Wallace Fowlie translations.

"Rimbaud on Rambo III" is a collage of phrases from Arthur Rimbaud's poems and letters from multiple translations by Wallace Fowlie, Wyatt Mason, Enid Peschel, Paul Schmidt, Martin Sorrell, and Louise Varese.